Table of contents

Introduction

In today's business environment, teams must innovate iteratively and quickly with ever decreasing allowances for time-to-market. They must align, innovate, collaborate, and execute seamlessly to maintain peak performance and achieve their goals – even as those goals shift.

These teams move fast, use minimal resources, and take informed risks with new ideas. In short, they build a climate and culture where people love to work and contribute.

When the leaders and members of teams better understand how to manage their dynamics to fit the situation, they can become generative. **That is, their productivity, creativity, and innovation increase exponentially in service of the mission and vision.** Individuals are more willing to contribute creatively beyond their own interests to serve something greater than themselves.

*T*ilt enables individuals and teams to become generative by creating healthy, innovative climates that keep the focus on generative results.

Generativity is competitive advantage!

Certification course objectives

After you have completed Team Agility Predictor Certification, you should be able to help teams:

- Identify their current assumptions and why they work the way they do
- Use selected *T*ilt patterns of team agility to develop more effective and productive ways of working together toward goals
- Quickly coach themselves, as a team, back to agility
- Build a plan for their development opportunities

Reflection

Given the Team Agility Predictor Certification workshop objectives, what do you most hope to learn during this workshop?

What is a team?

My peak team experience

What is the most rewarding team experience you have had?

What made it such a great team experience? Include as many specifics as you can.

Attributes of healthy team climates

Climate versus culture

Culture	Climate

What is the best way to change company culture and why? ______________________

____

Generative teams

Balance and flow – and generative team strategic model

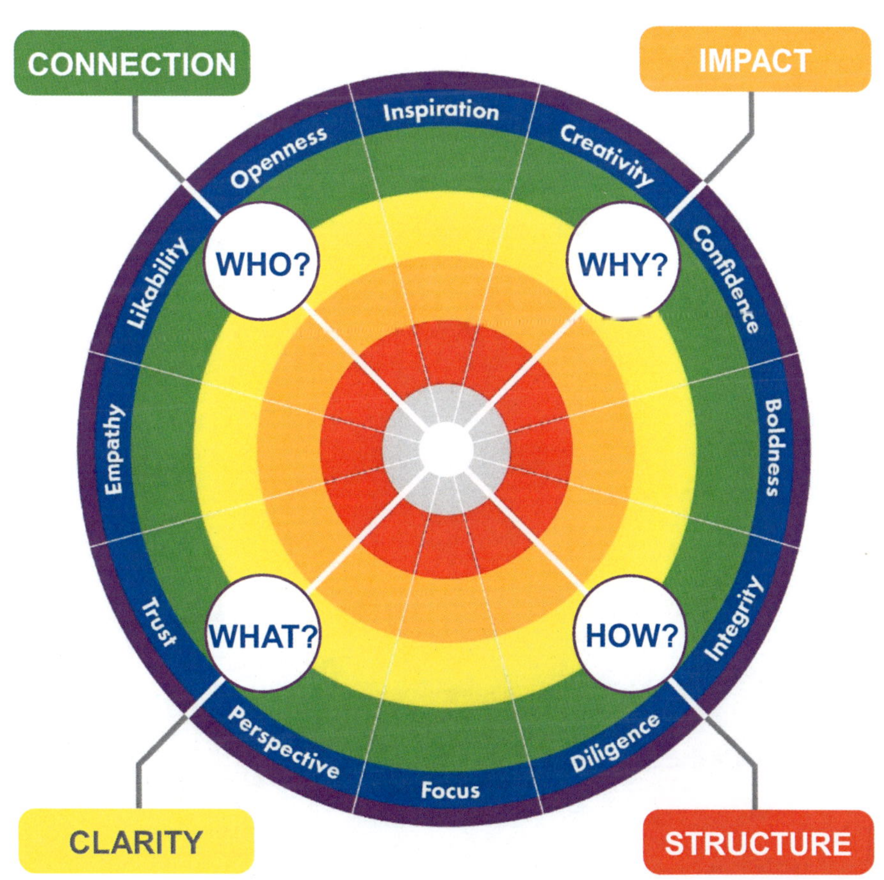

Flow

Agilities, polarities, balance, and flow

Character Strengths enable Agilities

The 12 Agilities

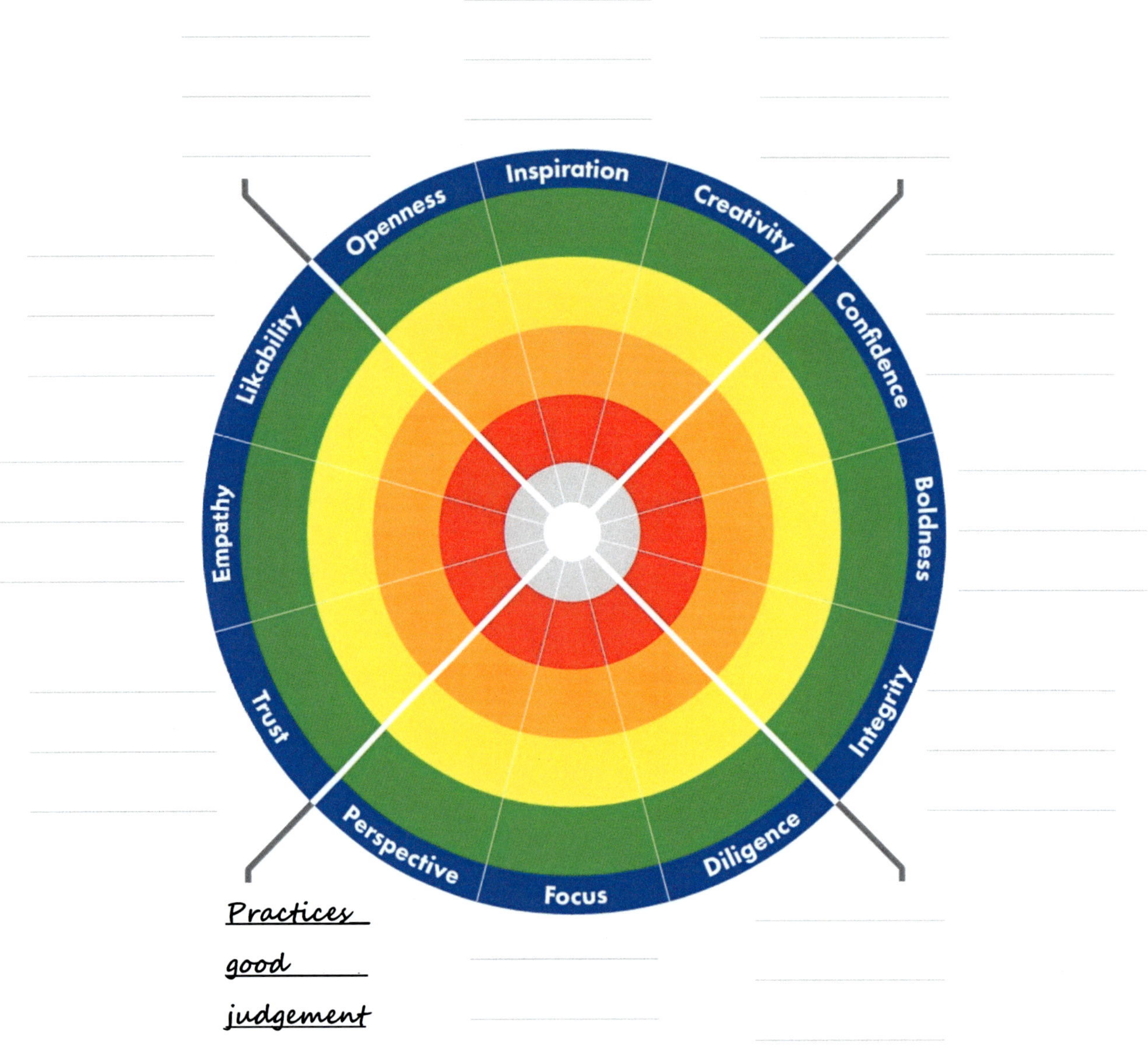

Tilt Factor Chart

THE 4 META FACTORS		CORE LEADERSHIP STRENGTHS	Under-Developed Traits	Commendable Traits	Over-Used Traits
WISDOM: HEAD	FACTS ▶ JUDGMENT	PERSPECTIVE Practices Good Judgment	Illogical Subjective Irrational Unrealistic	Logical Objective Rational Realistic	Robotic Scrutinizing Skeptical Paranoid
		FOCUS Attends to Priorities	Aimless Reactive Careless Undiscerning	Purposeful Mindful Selective Discerning	Intolerant Stoic Restrictive Critical
		DILIGENCE Effective at Execution	Unproductive Undisciplined Inconsistent Nonchalant	Productive Disciplined Consistent Conscientious	Workaholic Obsessive Rigid Meticulous
HUMANITY: HEART	PEOPLE ▶ HARMONY	LIKABILITY Expands Social Influence	Unapproachable Unappreciative Withholding Intense	Approachable Appreciative Generous Friendly	Permissive Flattering Indulgent Flippant
		EMPATHY Shows Emotional Awareness	Restless Rejecting Disrespectful Blaming	Patient Accepting Respectful Forgiving	Passive Adoring Submissive Excusing
		TRUST Builds Strong Relationships	Boastful Fickle Superficial Unreliable	Humble Loyal Authentic Reliable	Meek Resigned Transparent Compliant
COURAGE: GUT	ACTION ▶ JUSTICE	CONFIDENCE Exudes a Commanding Presence	Insecure Indecisive Uncertain Passive	Self-Assured Decisive Certain Assertive	Arrogant Dismissive Defensive Aggressive
		BOLDNESS Willing to Face Risk	Timid Cautious Unengaged Slack	Brave Adventurous Passionate Tenacious	Reckless Destructive Antagonistic Stubborn
		INTEGRITY Serves as a Good Example	Secretive Biased Unethical Political	Honest Fair Ethical Honorable	Blunt Patronizing Strict Judgmental
RESILIENCE: SPIRIT	IDEAS ▶ PURPOSE	OPENNESS Shows Curiosity for Learning	Unreceptive Complacent Inflexible Inattentive	Receptive Curious Flexible Alert	Chaotic Scattered Erratic Impulsive
		INSPIRATION Casts a Compelling Vision	Withdrawn Mundane Apathetic Pessimistic	Visionary Compelling Enthusiastic Optimistic	Grandiose Overzealous Hyperactive Impractical
		CREATIVITY Designs Inventive Solutions	Uninventive Calculated Unimaginative Dependent	Ingenious Intuitive Innovative Resourceful	Eccentric Opinionated Opportunistic Mischievous

Balancing polarities

During the debriefing, write the name of the polarity in the far left column.

Focus		What it would look like if a team was…
	Over–*T*ilted into casting a compelling vision:	
	Over–*T*ilted into attending to priorities:	
	BALANCED on this polarity	
	Over–*T*ilted into designing inventive solutions	
	Over–*T*ilted into practicing good judgment	
	BALANCED on this polarity	
	Over–*T*ilted into exuding a commanding presence	
	Over–*T*ilted into building strong relationships	
	BALANCED on this polarity	
	Over–*T*ilted into facing risk willingly	
	Over–*T*ilted into showing emotional awareness	
	BALANCED on this polarity	

Polarities and balance (continued)

Focus		What it would look like if a team was...
	Over–*T*ilted into serving as a good example	
	Over–*T*ilted into expanding social influence	
	BALANCED on this polarity	
	Over–*T*ilted into executing effectively	
	Over–*T*ilted into showing curiosity for learning	
	BALANCED on this polarity	

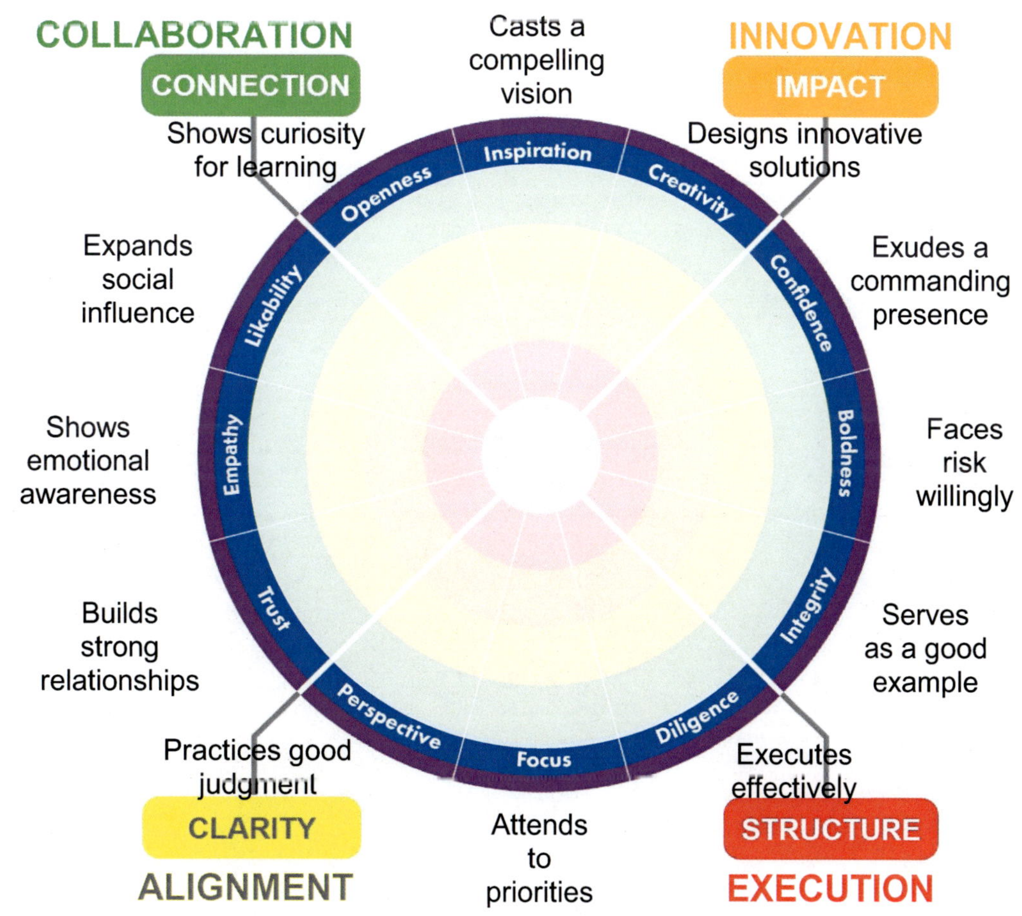

*T*ilt team assessments

Team Climate Profile

A Team Climate Profile is the compilation of the True *T*ilts of all members of a team.

What does the Team Climate Profile report tell us?

What does the Team Climate Profile report *not* tell us?

Additional notes:

Team climates

Connection Team Climate summary: Adaptive & Inclusive

Focus: Humanity & Resilience → People and Ideas

Values: Collaboration, inclusion, reputation, social influence, relationships, entertaining, beauty, serving others, caring for community, spreading good news and ideas, being open

Essence: Receptive optimism; "Everything always works out for the best, so we must bring everyone together to make the world a more pleasant, beautiful place in which to live."

Key team strengths:

- Brainstorms limitless possibilities
- Open to learning
- Spreads new ideas and trends
- Charming, likable
- Socially compelling and convincing
- Includes diverse ways and opinions

Potential pitfalls:

- Constant new ideas may lead to chaos, lack of decisiveness and follow–through
- May be optimistic without good reason
- Spreads new ideas and trends
- Can be naïve and exploited by others
- Focus on what others think can derail productivity and execution

Shift to higher effectiveness: Certain skepticism; "What if everyone doesn't always have good intentions and we need to protect ourselves from being exploited?"

Clarity Team Climate summary: Reflective & Analytical

Focus: Wisdom & Humanity → Data and People

Values: Alignment, integration, preparation, data and risk analysis, key metrics, investigation, patience, respect, mindfulness, research, historical reference

Essence: Receptive skepticism; "What we don't yet know could harm us, so we must be patient and delve into the details, which takes time."

Key team strengths:

- Makes meaning from / acts based on data
- Is always prepared, "does the homework" on diverse perspectives
- Builds trust
- Anticipates human cost and risks
- Troubleshoots and adapts well, "plan B"
- Is patient in making decision

Potential team pitfalls:

- Needs for analysis can delay progress, decisions, and influence
- Freezes when faced with high risk
- Holds back from voicing opinions and insights
- Seems lacking in confidence
- May be overly critical of those who are less competent

Shift to higher effectiveness: Certain optimism; "What if more data and analysis is just preventing us from being effective and we moved forward with what we know right now?"

Impact Team Climate summary: Competitive & Futuristic

Focus: **Resilience & Courage →** Ideas & Results

Values: Innovation, decisiveness, speed, application, usefulness, novelty, creativity, confidence, future–orientation

Essence: Certain optimism; "We know we are right and the future is ripe with opportunity, so we must catalyze change fast, before it's too late."

Key team strengths:

- Brings new and inventive ideas to reality
- "Powers through" difficulties; overcome challenges
- Appears highly competent and confident
- Inspires others and changes the future with big, creative thinking
- Intuits trends

Potential pitfalls:

- May disregard time, data, emotions, or human costs in pursuit of innovation
- May not "do the homework," leading to false starts and re-work
- Takes risks based on hunches rather than data or analysis
- Seems arrogant or self–important

Shift to higher effectiveness: Receptive skepticism; "What if we are not always right and we are more patient and listen with discernment so we don't create false starts?"

Structure Team Climate summary: Protective & Forceful

Focus: **Wisdom & Courage →** Results & Data

Values: Execution, efficiency, accuracy, conscientiousness, integrity, precision, quality, honesty, fairness, perfection, order, focus

Essence: Certain skepticism; "We know we are right, so we must be the ones to keep order and reduce potential harm."

Key team strengths:

- Makes sound decisions quickly
- Executes decisions efficiently
- Is highly responsible, focused and organized
- Provides reliability and consistency over the long term
- Ensures safety and sustainability

Potential pitfalls:

- Intense focus on the goal may result in missing new trends and ideas
- May shut off learning to "just execute"
- Uncomfortable with pivoting or changing the plan
- Is impatient with "too much" discussion, analysis, or off–task behavior
- Seems cold or unemotional

Shift to higher effectiveness: Receptive optimism; "What if we are not always right and we are more curious, intuitive, and open to social support?"

Team Agility Predictor

Science

Team's view

Leader's view

Entire data view

Notes on 'Million Dollar Team' exercise

Notes on *T*ilt Habits Discovery Card Sort

Developing sustainable generativity

A method for sustainable generativity

What is the goal?

Which *T*ilt outcome does the goal require?

***T*ilt outcomes** (net effect of the Agilities in the quadrants that make up the intentional *T*ilt)

COLLABORATION

Be open to new perspectives
Embrace possibilities
Learn from emergent trends
Make decisions collaboratively
Offer fresh solutions

INNOVATION

Break down barriers to change
Fail fast and learn quickly
Plow through obstacles
Think much bigger
Introduce game-changing ideas

ALIGNMENT

Define objectives & metrics clearly
Analyze risks & tradeoffs thoroughly
Make contingency plans
Provision resources to fit needs
Analyze data to guide decisions

EXECUTION

Time–box sprints to focus work
Architect a plan & prioritize
Be accountable for results
Use resources efficiently
Deliver high quality products

Which intentional Tilt will help us achieve the net effect (*T*ilt outcome)?

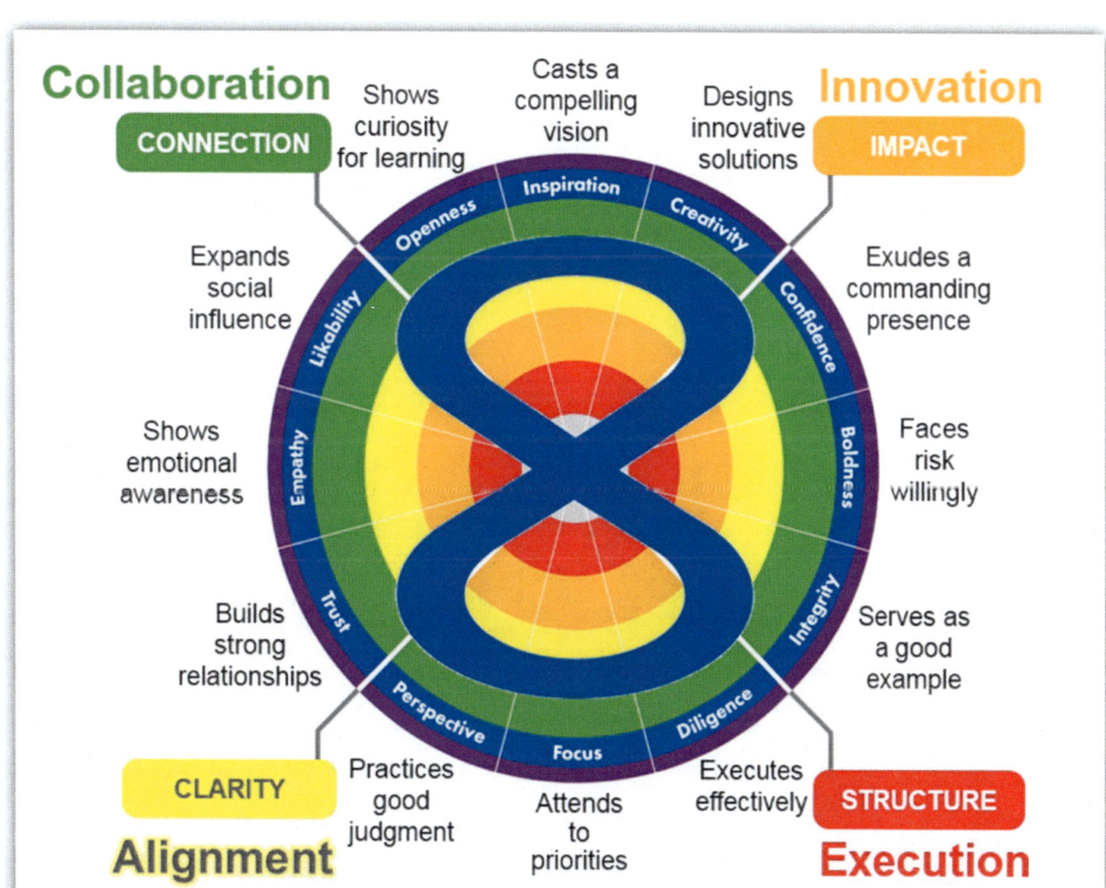

See Commitments of intentional *T*ilting on next page

What do team members need in order to maintain agile balance?

Commitments of intentional *T*ilting

- No surprises
- Say when and for how long you will be *T*ilting intentionally
- Say why the intentional *T*ilting is necessary
- Test every decision against the desired *T*ilt outcome in real time
- Give each other positive reinforcement (5-step process for getting back on the Agility Continuum)
- Team leader commits to working with a practitioner to learn how to help the team (and self) process stress

The Agility Continuum

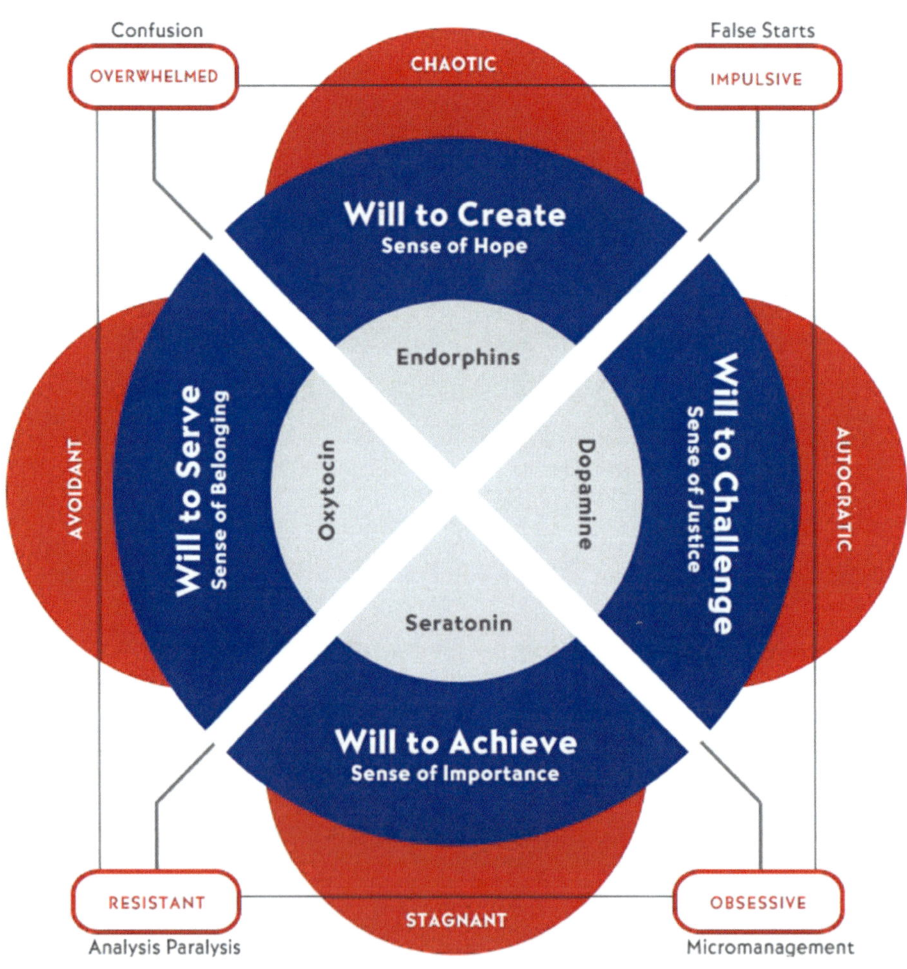

What to do when we drop off of the Continuum

Notice it → Name it → Process it → Decide → Redirect

Learn from a less–than–peak experience in a peak team

Briefly describe a situation that occurred in your "peak team" that stressed you out.

Notice it: How did you know that things were 'going downhill'?

Name it: Which stress reaction did you have?

Process it: What were you concerned about? What was driving this concern? How would you have liked to see it resolved?

Decide: What could the team have done to address the issue?

Redirect: What did the team need to do to get back into flow?

Planning to achieve goals

Our team agreements and development plan

Our goal:

The Tilt outcome the goal requires:

The intentional *T*ilt on which we all need to focus:

My personal plan:

What is likely to trigger stress in me?

What do I need when that happens?

My spotters will be:

How my spotters can help me:

TIP: Pull out this development plan, the *T*ilt outcomes image, and the Commitments of intentional *T*ilting. Post them near your desk for easy reference.

Call to Action

Agile

THE POSITIVE INFLUENCER

When you have developed balance in all of the character strengths on the Tilt Model, then you are able to lean into whatever is needed in a given context. When triggered, you self-regulate your own behavior so that you do not trigger reactionary behavior in others.

Top Question: Where should I Tilt right now?

Top Motivators: Balance and Flow

Top Character Strengths: Self regulation

Motivates You: Creative Contribution in your chosen domain.

Motivation Levers: Being in flow.

Demotivates You: Distraction from flow.

Best Pace: Whatever the current situation needs.

Wants from Others: Character development, so the team can be in flow.

Offers to Others: Model for behavior.

Top Emotions: Gratitude, fulfillment

Stress Reaction: The same as your True Tilt, but you can recover quickly.

Emotions Under Stress: The same as your True Tilt, but you can recover quickly.

Problematic Trait: The same as your True Tilt, but it's less likely to show up and you can recover from it quickly.

Motto: Be Kind, Be Wise, Be Bold, Be Unique, Be Real

Big Moves: What am I doing "big" in the world

Notes:

Connection

THE CROSS-POLLINATOR

Top outcome: Collaboration

Top question: Who?

Motivators: Socializing, storytelling

Wants from others: Freedom, diplomacy

Offers to others: Acceptance of differences

RESILIENCE

Driven by: IDEAS

Top character strengths:
Openness
Inspiration
Creativity

Needs: Attention and recognition

Inner stress reaction: FLEE

HUMANITY

Driven by: PEOPLE

Top character strengths:
Likability
Empathy
Trust

Needs: Approval and acceptance

Inner stress reaction: deFLECT

Motto: So many ideas, so many people, so little time

Best pace: Spontaneous, quick

Stress reaction: Overwhelmed; causes others confusion

Big moves: Be Wise – increase SKEPTICISM
Be Bold – increase CERTAINTY

When you are *T*ilting in CONNECTION, you appear to be focused on connecting PEOPLE and IDEAS, so you may be more alert to the needs of others and can intuit just how to help them. In this mode, you may feel more receptive than usual and can quickly interpret the cues to improvise. You may be focused on expanding social networks and positive influence to socialize your ideas.

Notes:

Impact

THE CHANGE CATALYST

RESILIENCE

Driven by: IDEAS

Top character strengths:
Openness
Inspiration
Creativity

Needs: Attention and recognition

Inner stress reaction: FLEE

Top outcome: Innovation

Top question: Why?

Motivators: Changing the world

Wants from others: Positivity, cooperation

Offers to others: Confidence, risk–taking

COURAGE

Driven by: RESULTS

Top character strengths:
Confidence
Boldness
Integrity

Needs: Power and autonomy

Inner stress reaction: FIGHT

Motto: Everything that tests me makes me feel alive

Best pace: Rocket speed

Stress reaction: Impulsivity; causes others false starts

Big moves: Be Kind – increase RECEPTIVITY
Be Wise – increase SKEPTICISM

When you are *T*ilting in IMPACT, you appear to be connecting IDEAS and RESULTS, so you may be inventing new solutions by linking seemingly disparate information into meaningful expressions of your creative imagination. You appear ready to take risks and want to drive a new idea into action quickly. You may have a pressing need to follow your gut instinct regarding your hunches.

Notes

Structure

THE MASTER MIND

COURAGE

Driven by: RESULTS

Top character strengths:
Confidence
Boldness
Integrity

Needs: Power and autonomy

Inner stress reaction: FIGHT

WISDOM

Driven by: DATA

Top character strengths:
Diligence
Focus
Perspective

Needs: Security and status

Inner stress reaction: FREEZE

Top outcome: Execution

Top question: How?

Motivators: Data, results

Wants from others: Autonomy, respect

Offers to others: Decisiveness, discipline

Motto: Efficiency and precision equal perfection

Best pace: Measured and efficient

Stress reaction: Obsession; others feel micromanaged

Big moves: Be Unique – increase OPTIMISM
Be Kind – increase RECEPTIVITY

When you are *T*ilting in STRUCTURE, you appear to be connecting RESULTS and DATA. You may be masterminding and building intricate, precise systems that offer stability and sustainability over time. You know how to focus on and execute work requiring complex reasoning and heavy task orientation, so you may appear a bit anti–social until the work is done.

Notes

Clarity

THE QUIET GENIUS

HUMANITY

Driven by: PEOPLE

Top character strengths:
Likability
Empathy
Trust

Needs: Approval and acceptance

Inner stress reaction: deFLECT

Top outcome: Alignment

Top question: What?

Motivators: Researching, supporting

Wants from others: Appreciation, kindness

Offers to others: Discernment, support

WISDOM

Driven by: DATA

Top character strengths:
Diligence
Focus
Perspective

Needs: Security and status

Inner stress reaction: FREEZE

Motto: It's better to prepare than to regret

Best pace: Patient, thoughtful

Stress reaction: Resistance; causes others analysis paralysis

Big moves: Be Bold – increase CERTAINTY
Be Unique – increase OPTIMISM

When you are *T*ilting in **CLARITY**, you appear to be connecting PEOPLE and IDEAS. You may be analyzing and interpreting data that ultimately affects others, so you are not ready to make decisions. As you investigate the details thoroughly and explore options, you may find yourself in an advisory role because others find your judgement credible and sense that they can trust you.

Made in United States
Orlando, FL
23 May 2023